To the B...

Lots of luv
Mum xx

THE LITTLE BOOK OF DIVAS

THE LITTLE BOOK OF DIVAS

Summersdale Publishers Ltd
46 West Street
Chichester
West Sussex
PO19 1RP
UK

www.summersdale.com

Printed and bound in China

ISBN: 978-1-84953-381-2

THE LITTLE BOOK OF
DIVAS

JENNY KEMPE

summersdale

INTRODUCTION

The world's biggest divas did not realise their unique talents by adhering to norms. They did not come into fame and money by trying to be liked or to fit in. From Mae West to Madonna, these women did it their own way. They stayed true to themselves and apologised to no one. Did they make the world a better place? Time will tell. In the meantime, they have made their mark. They have entertained, inspired and shown us that the very best thing you can be in this world is yourself.

The Little Book of Divas is a collection of my artwork matched with quotations by some of the world's most brilliant divas. I have selected the wittiest and most outlandish quotes about men, sex, cheating, shopping, diets, chocolate, wine and the meaning of life, to help you find and celebrate your own inner diva.

The Little Book of Divas is served tongue-in-cheek, and with a whole lot of attitude. I hope you will enjoy reading it as much as I did putting it together!

JENNY KEMPE

After all, Ginger Rogers did **EVERYTHING** that Fred Astaire did.

She just did it **BACKWARDS** and in high heels.

ANN RICHARDS

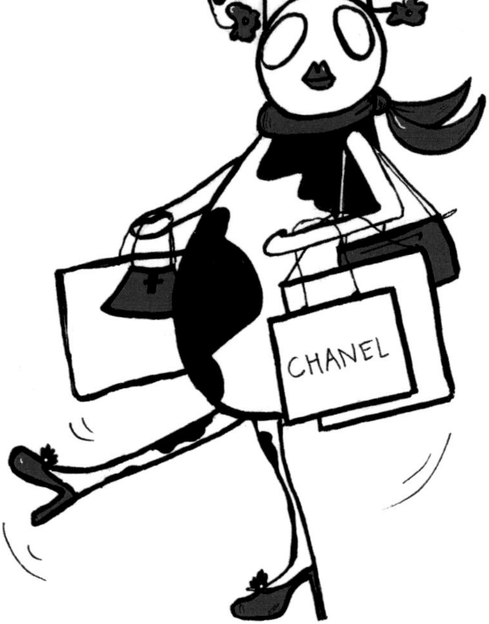
CHANEL

Whoever said money can't buy

HAPPINESS

simply didn't know where to go

SHOPPING.

BO DEREK

I have never hated

A MAN

enough

to give his

DIAMONDS

back.

ZSA ZSA GABOR

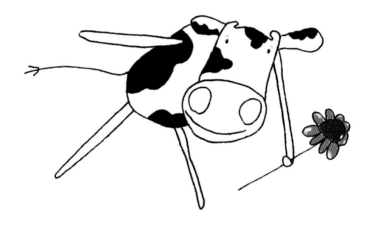

Never do **ANYTHING** yourself

that **OTHERS** can do for you.

AGATHA CHRISTIE

If you DON'T HAVE anything nice to say

about ANYONE...

come sit by me.

ALICE ROOSEVELT LONGWORTH

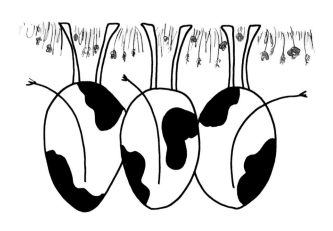

I have to

EXERCISE

in the morning

before my brain

FIGURES OUT

what I'm doing.

MARSHA DOBLE

The only thing
with doing nothing

is that you
NEVER KNOW
when you're finished.

ANONYMOUS

Whatever women do

THEY MUST

do twice as well as men

to be thought half

AS GOOD.

Luckily, this is not difficult.

CHARLOTTE WHITTON

I used to be

SNOW WHITE,

but I

DRIFTED.

MAE WEST

Lead me not into **TEMPTATION;** I can find the way **MYSELF.**

RITA MAE BROWN

The male is a domestic

ANIMAL

which, if treated with

firmness and kindness, can be

TRAINED

to do most things.

JILLY COOPER

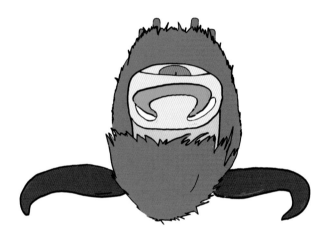

I don't do
FASHION!

I am
FASHION.

COCO CHANEL

I don't mean to be

A DIVA,

but some days

you wake up

AND YOU'RE

Barbra Streisand.

COURTNEY LOVE

You're as

as you

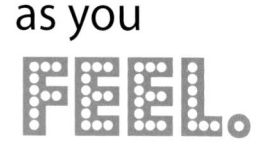

ELIZABETH ARDEN

I don't care what is

WRITTEN

about me

as long as it

ISN'T

true.

KATHARINE HEPBURN

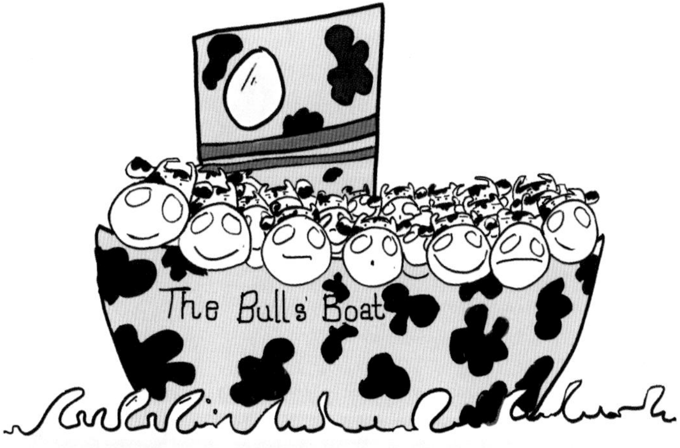
The Bulls' Boat

Love, like other **ARTS,** requires **EXPERIENCE.**

LADY CAROLINE LAMB

I don't

DIET.

I just don't eat as much as

I'D LIKE TO.

LINDA EVANGELISTA

The trouble with some

WOMEN

is that they get

all excited about

NOTHING

– and then marry him.

Everyone is

ENTITLED

to my

OPINION.

MADONNA

Instant gratification IS NOT soon ENOUGH.

MERYL STREEP

One more **DRINK** and I'd have

been **UNDER** the host.

DOROTHY PARKER

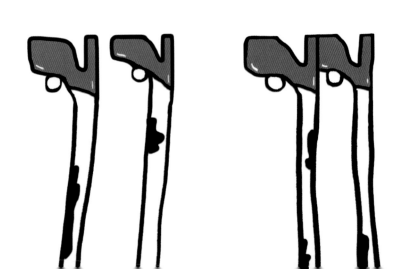

If high heels

WERE SO

wonderful,

men would

STILL BE

wearing them.

SUE GRAFTON

How many **HUSBANDS** have I had? You mean **APART FROM** my own?

ZSA ZSA GABOR

If God

WANTED

us to bend over

he'd put

DIAMONDS

on the floor.

JOAN RIVERS

Take your life in your **OWN HANDS,** and what happens?

A terrible thing: **NO ONE** to blame.

ERICA JONG

If I can't have too many

TRUFFLES,

I'll do without

TRUFFLES.

COLETTE

What I don't like about office

CHRISTMAS

parties

is looking for

A JOB

the next day.

PHYLLIS DILLER

There is so little

DIFFERENCE

between husbands

you might as well

KEEP

the first.

ADELA ROGERS ST JOHNS

Never drink BLACK COFFEE at lunch;

it will keep you AWAKE all afternoon.

JILLY COOPER

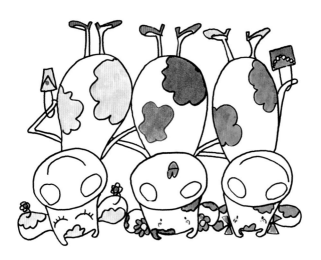

If you've got it,

FLAUNT IT.

If you don't,

ACCESSORISE.

ANONYMOUS

If I have the knack TO AMUSE the public,

I shall expect the public to be GRATEFUL to me.

HARRIETTE WILSON

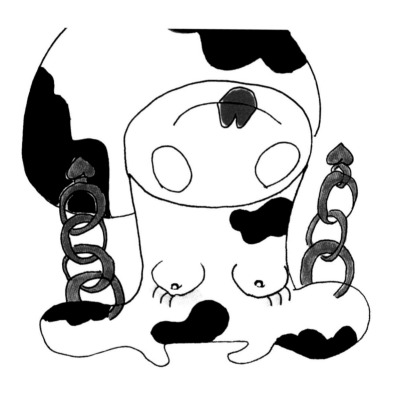

I generally avoid

TEMPTATION

unless

I can't

RESIST

it.

MAE WEST

I'm not offended by all the **DUMB BLONDE** jokes because I know

I'm not dumb… and I **ALSO KNOW** that I'm not blonde.

DOLLY PARTON

The important thing is

NOT WHAT

they think of me,

but what

I THINK

of them.

QUEEN VICTORIA

If love is the **ANSWER** could you please **REPHRASE** the question?

JANE WAGNER

My second-favorite HOUSEHOLD chore is ironing.

My first being hitting MY HEAD on the top bunk bed until I faint.

ERMA BOMBECK

I never know HOW MUCH of what I say IS TRUE.

BETTE MIDLER

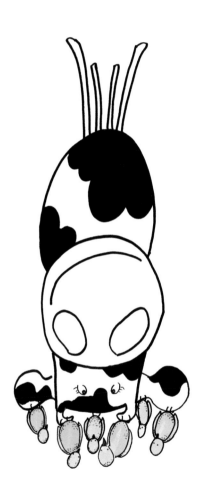

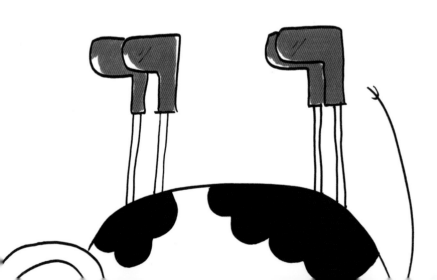

Husbands **COME** and go,

but Manolo Blahnik **SLINGBACKS** are for life.

LIZA MINNELLI

I love men, **EVEN THOUGH** they're lying, cheating **SCUMBAGS.**

GWYNETH PALTROW

It is **BETTER**

to be a

bad

ORIGINAL,

than a good copy.

MARQUISE DU DEFFAND

I have only two temperamental **OUTBURSTS** a year –

each **LASTS** six months.

TALLULAH BANKHEAD

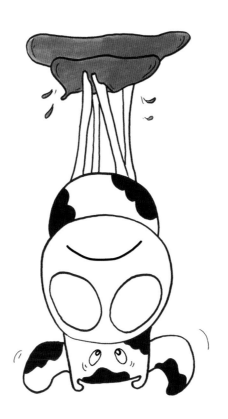

It's not
THE MEN
in your life that matters,

it's
THE LIFE
in your men.

MAE WEST

I finally **FIGURED OUT**
the only reason
to be alive is
TO ENJOY it.

RITA MAE BROWN

I want

A MAN

who's kind and understanding.

Is that too much

TO ASK

of a millionaire?

ZSA ZSA GABOR

Actually, I take it as a

COMPLIMENT.

Diva is a derivative of

CALISTA FLOCKHART

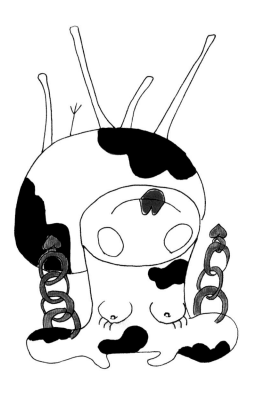

If you're interested in finding out more about our humour books, follow us on Twitter:
@SummersdaleLOL

www.summersdale.com